witches vanish

Also by Claudia Barnett

I Love You Terribly: Six Plays

No. 731 Degraw-street, Brooklyn, or Emily Dickinson's Sister: A Play in Two Acts

WITCHES VANISH

a play by CLAUDIA BARNETT

Carnegie Mellon University Press
Pittsburgh 2021

Book design by Stacey Hsi

Library of Congress Control Number 2020951046
ISBN 978-0-88748-665-4

10 9 8 7 6 5 4 3 2 1

for Julia Fesmire

and my weïrd sisters,
Diane Di Ianni, McAdoo Greer, and Valerie Hart

CONTENTS

My dearest daughter, at last I can write to you, now that I have a place to find you: Asteroid 11441, between Mars and Jupiter.

—Zaida Franz,
whose daughter Ana Teresa Diego was kidnapped in Argentina in 1976.
The asteroid Anadiego was named in her honor.

ACKNOWLEDGMENTS

Witches Vanish was sparked by a tableau: A young woman's decaying body lies on a coroner's table. Her grieving parents huddle beside her and stare at her boots. They remember when she bought them, how they'd disapproved of the color, the expense. Her father touches the red leather tenderly, then turns to his wife: "So skinny." The mother nods, agrees; the girl'd lost weight. She'd been missing for months. Then the mother looks closer and notices: Those are not her jeans. Not her shirt. Not her earrings. In fact, now that she's paying attention, she remembers: Her daughter was not this tall.

This image haunted me for years—since the first time I read Alma Guillermoprieto's "Letter from Mexico: A Hundred Women," subtitled "Why has a decade-long string of murders gone unsolved?" in *The New Yorker* in 2003. I kept the article filed away, knowing I would need it. When I reread it years later, I realized the boots were a product of my imagination, but the horror of the hundred missing women, their parents forced to identify unrecognizable remains, was entirely fact—and still is. In Ciudad Juárez, women are still disappearing, and the numbers are in the thousands.

I spent the summer of 2010 in Prague, surrounded by marionettes. There, I heard Ivan Klima lecture about *samizdat* and started thinking about disappearance in different ways. Several months later, as I was writing a proposal for a residency at a Chicago theater, I suddenly realized the connections between vanishing women, silenced voices, and puppets. That's how *Witches Vanish* began.

Many talented and generous artists have contributed to the development of *Witches Vanish*. I'm deeply grateful to all. I must single out a few:

Scott Bishop, an ensemble member at Stage Left Theatre, began directing this play even before it was written and brought my vision to life. Actors Julie Cowden, Cat Dean, Ashlee Edgemon, Kimberly Logan, and Kristen Secrist made invaluable contributions, as did puppet consultant Matt Rudy and everyone at Stage Left who supported this play's development for nearly a year. The creation of *Witches Vanish* was a true collaboration.

Director Melissa Maxwell guided several revisions of the script. Dramaturgs Mary Vingoe and Heather Helinsky inspired major improvements. Artistic directors Vance Smith, Lorca Peress, Ruth Lawrence, and Kevin Lawler and literary manager Zev Valancy believed in the play and paired me with ideal partners.

I also wish to thank director Deborah Randall and the cast of the Venus Theatre production for their ingenuity, talent, unflagging commitment, and physical exertion. Neil McFadden's eerie soundscape of names still plays in my memory. Deb's addition of the Shadow Witches made this "impossible play" possible.

I very much appreciate the support of my home institution, Middle Tennessee State University, including the Faculty Development Committee, the Faculty Research & Creative Activity Committee, the College of Liberal Arts, the College of Graduate Studies, the Women's and Gender Studies Program, and the English Department.

Scene 3: "Swimming in the Afternoon" was published in *River Styx* 93.
Scene 8: "Kilometer 14" was published in *Poems & Plays* 21.

DEVELOPMENT HISTORY

Witches Vanish was originally developed through the Downstage Left development program at Stage Left Theatre, Chicago, 2011, directed by Scott Bishop.

Witches Vanish had a workshop production as part of LeapFest 9: A Downstage Left Festival of New Plays, Stage Left Theatre, Chicago, 2012, directed by Scott Bishop.

Witches Vanish was a finalist for the MultiStages New Works Contest and had a staged reading as part of the MultiStages New Works Finalist Festival, Multi-Stages, New York, 2014, directed by Melissa Maxwell.

Witches Vanish had a staged reading at the Eighth Annual Women's Work Festival, St. John's, Newfoundland, Canada, 2014, directed by Mary Vingoe.

Witches Vanish had a staged reading at the Great Plains Theatre Conference, Omaha, Nebraska, 2014, directed by Julia Hinson.

Witches Vanish had a staged reading by Venus Theatre at the 13th Annual Page-to-Stage New Play Festival at the John F. Kennedy Center for the Performing Arts, Washington, D.C., 2014, directed by Deborah Randall.

Witches Vanish received its world premiere at Venus Theatre (Deborah Randall, artistic director) on August 20, 2015, as part of the Women's Voices Theater Festival. Deborah Randall directed. Lights were designed by Kristin Thompson, sound by Neil McFadden, sets and costumes by Deborah Randall. Set design was by Amy Belschner-Rhodes and marketing by Laura Matteoni Schraven.

WITCH 1	Lakeisha Harrison
WITCH 2	Vivian Allvin
WITCH 3	Tara Cariaso
SHADOW WITCH 1*	Jennifer Berry
SHADOW WITCH 2*	Leticia Monet

* For the Venus production of *Witches Vanish*, director Deborah Randall added two Shadow Witches to the cast. These masked creatures silently created the world of the play and functioned as the cauldron.

WITCHES VANISH

CHARACTERS

WITCH 1
WITCH 2
WITCH 3

The characters are the witches from Shakespeare's *Macbeth*, only beautiful and beardless. They play all the other roles in this play. Their default costumes are black cocktail dresses.

TIME
The time is the past and the present.

PLACE
The setting is an empty space dominated by an enormous cauldron.

NOTES
The lists of names in the transitions were first created to facilitate scene changes; they grew into a chilling choral refrain. Directors are encouraged to expand and update the lists. I imagine the Witches clearing the stage with red push brooms and then setting up the next scenes as they chant the names. I've been asked by directors to create bridges between the scenes; with the exception of the *Macbeth* moments and the Angélica crossings, please take these as suggestions.

The casting of the Venus production, which is reflected throughout this script, was as follows. Directors may cast the play as they see fit.

WITCH 1

SCENE 1 (La Cenicienta, part 1)	Fairy Godmother
SCENE 2 (Hellbroth)	Estrella, Soviet police, Inquisitor
SCENE 3 (Swimming)	Milena
SCENE 4 (La Cenicienta, part 2)	Factory worker
SCENE 5 (Lupus)	Narrator
SCENE 6 (Olive)	Beatriz
SCENE 7 (Aimée)	Pirate
SCENE 8 (K14)	Manya
SCENE 9 (4x)	Mother
SCENE 10 (La Cenicienta, part 3)	Estrellita

WITCH 2

SCENE 1 (La Cenicienta, part 1)	Angélica
SCENE 2 (Hellbroth)	Coroner, Maya, Inquistor
SCENE 3 (Swimming)	Olinka
SCENE 4 (La Cenicienta, part 2)	Angélica
SCENE 5 (Lupus)	Wolf
SCENE 6 (Olive)	Inés
SCENE 7 (Aimée)	Aimée
SCENE 8 (K14)	Mammoth
SCENE 9 (4x)	Chanthavy (doll)
SCENE 10 (La Cenicienta, part 3):	Angélica

WITCH 3

SCENE 1 (La Cenicienta, part 1)	Mother
SCENE 2 (Hellbroth)	Coroner, Soviet police, Cristina
SCENE 3 (Swimming)	Evka
SCENE 4 (La Cenicienta, part 2)	Whistle-blower
SCENE 5 (Lupus)	Red

OVERTURE

As the audience enters: The cauldron boils. Above it hangs a circle of rag dolls, suspended from a wheel, all facing the audience. The wheel revolves, and now and then, as the WITCHES chant the names, a doll falls into the pot. The WITCHES wear costumes and masks and appear as grotesque as Banquo describes them: "So wither'd and so wild in their attire, / That look not like the inhabitants o' the earth." THEY take turns stirring as THEY toss ingredients into the cauldron.

WITCHES

Eleanor Dare, age 27, and Virginia Dare, age 3.
Vanished from Roanoke, Virginia. 1590.

Theodosia Burr Alston, daughter of Vice President Aaron Burr, age 29.
Vanished at sea. 1813.

Dorothy Arnold, age 25.
Vanished from New York City. 1910.

Mildred Doran, "the flying schoolmarm," age 22.
Vanished at the Pacific Air Race. 1927.

Amelia Earhart, age 39.
Vanished flying over the Pacific. 1937.

Paula Jean Welden, age 18.
Vanished near Glastenbury Mountain, Vermont. 1946.

Robin Graham, age 18.
Ran out of gas on a California Highway. 1970.

Katherine Mary Lyon, age 10, and Sheila Mary Lyon, age 12.
Vanished from Washington, D.C. 1975.

Helen Dymond, age 48.
Vanished while walking home one night in National Mine, Michigan.
1981.

Anthonette Cayedito, age 9.
Vanished from her home in Gallup, New Mexico. 1986.

Patricia Adkins, age 29.
Vanished moments after punching out at midnight in Maryville,
Ohio. 1991.

Sherrill Levitt, age 47, Suzie Streeter, age 19, and Stacy McCall,
age 18, together known as "the Springfield Three."
Vanished from Springfield, Missouri. 1992.

Kristin Smart, age 19.
Vanished from California Polytechnic State University. 1996.

Kristen Modafferi, age 18.
Vanished from a mall in San Francisco. 1997.

Florinda Donner, age 54.
Vanished from California. 1998.

Amy Lynn Bradley, age 23.
Vanished from the cruise ship *Rhapsody of the Seas* as it was docking in
Antilles. 1998.

Maura Murray, age 21.
Vanished from the University of Massachusetts at Amherst. 2004.

Natalee Holloway, age 18.
Vanished from Oranjestad, Aruba. 2005.

Susan Cox Powell, age 28.
Vanished from West Valley City, Utah. 2009.

Stacey Coldon, age 23.
Vanished from her Chevy Blazer in St. Louis. 2011.

Jhessye Shockley, age 5.
Vanished from her home in Glendale, Arizona. 2011.

Robyn Gardner, age 35.
Vanished from Oranjestad, Aruba. 2011.

Tiffany Daniels, age 25.
Vanished from Pensacola Beach, Florida. 2013.

Maureen Kelly, age 19.
Vanished after leaving for a spiritual quest in the Gifford Pinchot National Forest. 2013.

Merrilee Cooley, age 68.
Vanished from her home in Clackamas, Oregon. 2016.

Kristal Reisinger, age 29.
Vanished from her home in Crestone, Colorado. 2016.

Deniece Brantley, age 37.
Vanished in San Antonio, Texas. 2017.

Anesha "Duffy" Murnane, age 38.
Vanished on her way to a wellness clinic in Homer, Alaska. 2019.

The last doll falls into the pot. Suddenly, the WITCHES tear off their costumes and masks, revealing their cocktail dresses. The play begins.

SCENE 1

LA CENICIENTA (PART 1)

*Her story reminds the child . . . how lucky [s]he is, and how much worse
things could be.*

—Bruno Bettelheim, *The Uses of Enchantment*

CHARACTERS

WITCH 1, WITCH 3   *Cocktail dresses.*
ANGÉLICA   *12.*

SETTING

The cauldron (center).

AT RISE

*WITCH 2 transforms into Angélica and sits on the floor. WITCHES 1 AND 3
reach into the cauldron for a dilapidated Barbie doll and a two-headed rag doll,
which THEY hand to Angélica as THEY exit. ANGÉLICA plays with the dolls.*

ANGÉLICA

Once upon a time there lived a girl named la Cenicienta who had two
horrible mean sisters who made her do all their chores and sleep in
the ashes.

> *ANGÉLICA holds up the Barbie doll as la Cenicienta
> and the rag doll as the stepsisters. SHE enacts the story
> with the dolls as she speaks.*

No one knew how pretty la Cenicienta was because she was always
dirty and tired. She spent her days chasing chickens and picking

chili peppers, while her sisters went to school and learned to dance. Then one day, the Prince announced a ball. The mean sisters told la Cenicienta to sew them dresses. Because her fingers were little, and because she had a lot of patience, she was an expert seamstress. Her sisters could not hide how delighted they were with the results. But then la Cenicienta was even tireder than usual because she stayed up all night sewing, and she was sad because her life was dull, so when she was picking chili peppers, she started to cry. Her sisters noticed the peppers were wet and salty, so they asked:

    (Mean-sister voice.)

"What's wrong, la Cenicienta?"

And she said,

    (Barbie voice.)

"I want to go to the ball."

And they laughed and laughed and poured a sack of lentils into the ashes. La Cenicienta got to work with her little fingers and plucked out every single lentil. She brought the lentils to her sisters, and they laughed and laughed and said,

    (Mean-sister voice.)

"That just proves you should be our maid. And besides, we prefer garbanzo beans."

Then they hurried off to catch the bus to the city.

    ANGÉLICA tosses the rag doll into the cauldron.

La Cenicienta stayed home and cried, dreaming of the Prince's ball. Then suddenly, her fairy godmother appeared and said . . .

    WITCH 3 enters. SHE wears a sombrero and an apron and carries a tiny suitcase.

WITCH 3

    Angélica, it's time to go. Your father and I have decided: We don't have enough to feed you, so we are sending you to Juárez to work in a *maquiladora*. We will miss you, but we know you will be happy, and you will learn important skills.

ANGÉLICA

(Holding up the Barbie doll.)

And la Cenicienta said . . .

WITCH 3

Angélica? Are you listening to me?

ANGÉLICA

(Barbie voice.)

Yes, fairy godmother. I have been a good girl, and you are sending me to the ball!

WITCH 3

I am sending you to the *maquiladora*.

ANGÉLICA

(Twirling the Barbie doll.)

Where I will dance with the Prince all night, and he will see I am the prettiest, and he will marry me in a fancy wedding.

WITCH 3

Angélica!

ANGÉLICA

(Her own voice.)

Yes, Mamá?

WITCH 3

You're not getting married. You are going to work.

ANGÉLICA

Yes, Mamá.

WITCH 3

I have packed your clothes.

SHE hands the suitcase to Angélica.

Let us walk to the bus stop together.

> *WITCH 3 grabs the Barbie doll and tosses it into the cauldron.*

ANGÉLICA

Mamá!

WITCH 3

You don't need dolls anymore, Angélica.

ANGÉLICA

Because I'm all grown up?

WITCH 3

That's right. You're all grown up.

ANGÉLICA

And I'm going to dance with the Prince?

> *WITCH 3 steers Angélica as THEY exit together. After a moment, WITCH 1 appears, wearing a crown of stars and holding a magic wand.*

WITCH 1

Angélica? It's me. Your fairy godmother. I've come to turn your lizards into footmen, your mice into horses, and your pumpkin into a golden coach.

> *Silence. WITCH 1 looks around and shrugs.*

I hate it when they change the script.

> *WITCH 1 waves her wand and vanishes.*

END OF SCENE 1

TRANSITION

The WITCHES chant (perhaps offstage):

Maria Elena Garcia Salas, age 18.
Vanished from Juárez, Mexico. December 5, 1995.

Veronica Muñoz Andrade, age 17.
Vanished from Juárez, Mexico. January 25, 1996.

Rosina Blanco Ramos, age 26.
Vanished from Juárez, Mexico. January 26, 1996.

Elena Guadian Simental, age 19.
Vanished from Juárez, Mexico. March 22, 1997.

Silvia Arcee, age 29.
Vanished from Juárez, Mexico. March 12, 1998.

Maria del Rosario Palacios Moran, age 18.
Vanished from Juárez, Mexico. December 7, 1998.

Carmen Cervantes Terrazas, age 42.
Vanished from Juárez, Mexico. May 1, 1999.

Elizabeth Rodriguez Perez, age 33.
Vanished from Juárez, Mexico. November 18, 1999.

SCENE 2

HELLBROTH

Come, sisters, cheer we up his sprites,
And show the best of our delights.
I'll charm the air to give a sound,
While you perform your antic round . . .

—William Shakespeare, *Macbeth*

CHARACTERS

WITCH 1, WITCH 2, WITCH 3.

SETTING

The cauldron (center).

AT RISE

The cauldron boils. WITCH 1 stirs as WITCHES 2 AND 3 dance and toss
ingredients into the pot.

WITCH 1
      Round about the cauldron go;
      In the poison'd entrails throw;
      Toad, that under cold stone
      Days and nights has thirty-one
      Swelt'red venom sleeping got,
      Boil thou first i' th' charmed pot.

ALL
      Double, double, toil and trouble;
      Fire burn, and cauldron bubble.

The WITCHES cackle. The cauldron stops steaming. WITCH 3 pulls a factory worker's smock out of the cauldron and hands it to WITCH 1, who puts it on over her dress. WITCH 1 walks in circles around the cauldron and transforms into ESTRELLA, who approaches Witches 2 and 3.

ESTRELLA

Por favor. They said I should talk to you. To find my Estrellita.

WITCH 3 pulls two lab coats out of the cauldron, keeps one for herself and hands the other to Witch 2. THEY put the lab coats on over their dresses. WITCH 3 removes a clipboard and pen from the cauldron and hands them to WITCH 2, who takes notes throughout the following exchange.

WITCH 3

Estrellita?

WITCH 2

Your star?

ESTRELLA

Mija. My daughter. One day last month, she never came home. I search for her every day.

WITCH 3

Age?

ESTRELLA

Sixteen. She is young and very beautiful. She loves ice cream. Strawberry best. She ate some on her birthday.

WITCH 2

Did she have a boyfriend?

WITCH 3

How many boyfriends?

WITCH 2

Why was she out at night?

ESTRELLA

No, no. Estrellita is a good girl. She worked at the *maquiladora*. They changed her hours and made her stay late at night. There was no bus to take her home.

WITCH 3

How was she dressed last time you saw her?

ESTRELLA

A blouse, red. A skirt, white. And sneakers.

> *WITCH 3 stirs the cauldron.*

WITCH 2

How short was the skirt?

WITCH 3

How tight was the shirt?

> *WITCH 3 pulls a pair of white tennis shoes from the cauldron and holds them up high. They have red laces.*

WITCH 2

Were these her sneakers?

ESTRELLA

Yes. I think so. *Dios mio.* She loved red laces.

> *WITCH 3 tosses the tennis shoes across the stage and pulls a white skirt from the cauldron. SHE holds it up high.*

WITCH 3

>Was this her skirt?

ESTRELLA

>She sewed it herself.

>>*ESTRELLA begins to cry. WITCH 3 tosses the skirt across the stage and pulls a red shirt from the cauldron. SHE holds it up high.*

WITCH 2

>Was this her blouse?

ESTRELLA

>*Sí.* I gave it to her at Christmas.

>>*ESTRELLA reaches for the blouse, but WITCH 3 tosses it across the stage. WITCH 3 reaches into the cauldron and pulls out a human skull, which SHE holds up high.*

WITCH 3

>Was this her head?

ESTRELLA

>*(SHE screams.)*
>*Mi bebe!*

>>*ESTRELLA grabs the skull and clutches it to her chest. After a moment, SHE examines the skull in her hands.*

What big teeth! No, it is not Estrellita. These teeth are not hers. Estrellita's are small. I would know my baby. She has pretty, little teeth.

WITCH 2

>Lacking the flesh and tissue normally associated with the face, the teeth may appear abnormally large.

ESTRELLA

> No. This is not my daughter. Estrellita is alive.

WITCH 3

> We are sorry for your loss.

ESTRELLA

> So many girls have disappeared in Juárez, and no one knows where they are. The police don't help. The government won't help. *Mija* is missing. I need your help. Please. You must conduct a test. DNA.

WITCH 2

> I'm afraid that won't be possible. You'll just have to trust us.

ESTRELLA

> Trust you, *señoras?*

WITCH 3

> What choice do you have?

> > *WITCH 1 collects the scattered clothing and clutches it to her chest, along with the skull. Suddenly, SHE tosses everything—the clothing, the skull, and her own smock— into the cauldron, which starts steaming. SHE is no longer Estrella. WITCH 2 tosses the lab coats, clipboard, and pen into the cauldron. WITCH 2 stirs while WITCHES 1 AND 3 dance. The cauldron steams.*

WITCH 2

> Fillet of a fenny snake,
> In the cauldron boil and bake;
> Eye of newt and toe of frog,
> Wool of bat and tongue of dog,
> Adder's fork and blind-worm's sting,
> Lizard's leg and howlet's wing,
> For a charm of pow'rful trouble,
> Like a hell-broth boil and bubble.

ALL

> Double, double, toil and trouble;
> Fire burn, and cauldron bubble.

> *The WITCHES cackle. The cauldron stops steaming.*
> *WITCH 1 pulls a thin, patched pink coat out of the*
> *cauldron and hands it to WITCH 2, who puts it on*
> *over her dress. WITCH 2 walks in circles around the*
> *cauldron and transforms into Maya, a shy little girl with*
> *her head hung down. MAYA approaches Witches 1 and*
> *3. WITCH 1 pulls a wrapped piece of candy from the*
> *cauldron and hands it to Maya.*

MAYA

> *Spasiba.*

> *WITCH 1 pulls two fur hats out of the cauldron.*
> *WITCHES 1 AND 3 put them on. MAYA is obviously*
> *cold and scared, but SHE is looking for something.*

WITCH 1

> That's all the candy you're getting. Now shoo.

MAYA

> *Puzhalsta . . .*

WITCH 3

> No more candy. It's bad for your teeth. It has eyes of newts in it. Hasn't
> your mother told you that?

MAYA

> My mother . . . *puzhalsta . . .*

WITCH 1

> What's your name, little girl?

MAYA

> My name is Maya.

WITCH 3

What do you want?

MAYA

I want my mother.

WITCH 1

Are you lost?

WITCH 3

Is she lost?

MAYA

Please. Do not take her away.

WITCH 1

Take her away?

WITCH 3

We don't take away mothers.

WITCH 1

We take away criminals.

WITCH 3

Enemies of the people. Politicals.

WITCH 1

We have a long list of politicals.

WITCH 3

One stole a spool of thread.

WITCH 1

One studied Esperanto.

WITCH 3

One asked the price of a bus ticket.

WITCH 1

> One danced the foxtrot.

MAYA

> My mother did not do that.

WITCH 3

> One perpetrated a facial crime.

MAYA

> What does that mean?

WITCH 1

> She smiled at Stalin's moustache.

MAYA

> My mother does not smile.

WITCH 3

> One stole potatoes from the field after harvest.

MAYA

> The potatoes? They were frozen in the field. No one wanted them.
> Mama collected them in the cold. . . . Her fingers turned blue.

WITCH 1

> Those potatoes belonged to the state.

WITCH 3

> Has she taught you to steal from the state?

MAYA

> No, please. Please give me back my mother. I'll give back the potatoes.

WITCH 3

> What's that you have in your hand? Candy?

> *SHE grabs the candy from Maya, unwraps it, and shows*
> *the wrapper to Witch 1.*

WITCH 1

> *Japanese* candy.

WITCH 3

> She must be a spy.

WITCH 1

> We'll send her to Siberia.

WITCH 3

> Like her mother.

MAYA

> Nooooooooooooooooooooooooo!

> *WITCH 2 tears off her coat and tosses it into the cauldron. SHE is no longer Maya. Meanwhile, WITCHES 1 AND 3 chuck the candy and the fur caps into the cauldron. WITCH 3 stirs while WITCHES 1 AND 2 dance. The cauldron steams.*

WITCH 3

> Scale of dragon, tooth of wolf,
> Witches' mummy, maw and gulf
> Of the ravin'd salt-sea shark,
> Root of hemlock digg'd i' th' dark,
> Liver of blaspheming Jew,
> Gall of goat, and slips of yew
> Silver'd in the moon's eclipse,
> Nose of Turk and Tartar's lips,
> Finger of birth-strangled babe
> Ditch-deliver'd by a drab,
> Make the gruel thick and slab.
> Add thereto a tiger's chawdron,
> For th' ingredients of our cau'dron.

ALL

> Double, double, toil and trouble;
> Fire burn, and cauldron bubble.

The WITCHES cackle. The cauldron stops steaming. WITCH 3 grabs a scarf from the cauldron, wraps it around her head, and walks in circles around the cauldron as SHE transforms into Cristina. WITCH 2 lifts three red crosses from the cauldron, each on a long chain. SHE puts one around WITCH 1's neck and two around her own. SHE removes a jar of water from the cauldron. SHE dances with WITCH 1. CRISTINA approaches Witches 1 and 3.

CRISTINA

Is this the Promised Land?
   (Singing in Hebrew.)
L'shana habaah b'yerushalayim . . .

WITCH 2 uncaps the jar and violently splashes the water in Cristina's face.

WITCH 2

I baptize you in the name of the Father, and of the Son, and the Holy Ghost.

CRISTINA

No. You've made a mistake. I can't be baptized; I'm a Jewess. From Castile. My name is Tziyona.

WITCH 1

Not anymore. Your name's Cristina.

CRISTINA

I must go home.

WITCH 2 removes one of the crosses from her own neck and places it over Cristina's head. CRISTINA grabs the cross and tries to take it off, but WITCHES 1 AND 2 stand ominously close.

CRISTINA

I can't wear this. I'm Jewish.

WITCH 2

Not anymore.

WITCH 1

There's no going back.

WITCH 2

You'll follow the rules of the Church.

WITCH 1

Or burn at the stake.

CRISTINA

I must go home. My family . . .

WITCH 1

You may not associate with Jews.

CRISTINA

My baby Ester, two years old.

WITCH 2

You may not speak with them.

WITCH 1

You may not pray with them.

WITCH 2

You may not dress like them.

SHE pulls the scarf off Cristina's head.

CRISTINA

They're expecting me for dinner.

WITCH 2

> You may not eat their foods.

WITCH 1

> You may not salt your meat.

WITCH 2

> Or trim its fat.

WITCH 1

> Or let its blood.

WITCH 2

> You must eat pork.

WITCH 1

> And eel.

WITCH 2

> And octopus.

WITCH 1

> You must not clean for Sabbath.

WITCH 2

> Or Pesach.

WITCH 1

> And don't apologize on Yom Kippur.

CRISTINA

> I'm sorry. I can't do that.

WITCH 2

> Then you'll burn at the stake for heresy.

CRISTINA

> I'm not a heretic. I'm a Jew.

> *WITCH 1 pulls the chain tightly around Cristina's neck, nearly choking her.*

WITCH 1

It's heretical to say so.

WITCH 2

You've been baptized.

WITCH 1

You'll be burned.

> *WITCH 1 removes a lighter and some branches from the cauldron as WITCH 2 pulls the chain around Cristina's neck and makes her stand straight, as if tied to a stake.*

CRISTINA

Please let me go home.

WITCH 2

You can't go home.

WITCH 1

You have no home.

> *WITCH 2 lays the branches in front of Cristina. WITCH 1 lights a match.*

CRISTINA

Oh no. I'm lost . . .

WITCH 2

Yes? Did you say lost?

WITCH 1

Have you lost a loved one?

WITCH 2
> Your mother?

WITCH 1
> Your daughter?

WITCH 2
> Yourself?

CRISTINA
> I wish I could vanish.

WITCH 1
> Can't you?

WITCH 2
> We can.

> *WITCH 1 blows out the match. WITCHES 1 AND 2 cackle and dance around the cauldron. THEY toss their crosses into the cauldron, which steams, and suddenly THEY vanish.*

CRISTINA
> This is not the Promised Land.

> *WITCH 3 removes the cross from around her neck and throws it into the cauldron. SHE is no longer Cristina.*

WITCH 3
> Poof.

> *SHE vanishes.*

END OF SCENE 2

TRANSITION

The WITCHES appear.

WITCH 1

> When shall we three meet again?
> In thunder, lightning, or in rain?

WITCH 2

> When the hurly-burly's done,
> When the battle's lost and won.

WITCH 3

> That will be ere the set of sun.

> *The WITCHES cackle as they chant the names, push*
> *the cauldron to the corner, and perform the actions that*
> *follow:*

Megumi Yokota, age 13.
Vanished from Niigata, Japan. 1977.

Emanuela Orlandi, age 15.
Vanished from Vatican City. 1983.

Madeleine McCann, age 3.
Vanished from Algarve, Portugal. 2007.

Amy Fitzpatrick, age 15.
Vanished from Málaga, Spain. 2008.

Nornabila Mat Yaacob, age 15.
Vanished from Kuantan, Malaysia. 2012.

Tameka Arika Absalon, age 15.
Vanished from Flat Rock, St. George, Barbados. 2012.

WITCH 2 exits. WITCH 1 lies down and transforms into Milena (asleep).

Four ropes descend from a crossbar that looms above the stage. WITCH 3 ties the ropes around Milena's ankles. SHE takes a white sheet from the cauldron and lays it over Milena.

As WITCH 3 exits, ANGÉLICA enters from the opposite direction. SHE crosses the stage, skipping happily and holding her tiny suitcase.

ANGÉLICA

I am on my way to the prince's ball, where I will dance all night!

SHE skips away.

SCENE 3

SWIMMING IN THE AFTERNOON

Germany has declared war on Russia. Swimming in the afternoon.

—Franz Kafka's diary, 2 August 1914

CHARACTERS

MILENA	*Balloon-bellied. Wears white.*
EVKA	*Old. White apron.*
OLINKA	*A marionette. Two feet tall. Red.*

SETTING

A crossbar that looks almost like a ceiling fan looms above the center of the stage. From it hang ropes tied to Milena's wrists and ankles. In a corner, the cauldron.

AT RISE

MILENA lies on her back on the floor, covered by a white sheet, her belly high in the air. After a moment, the ropes tug and lift her legs and arms. EVKA enters and pulls the sheet off Milena with a dramatic flourish.

EVKA

Wake up, Milena!

MILENA

Would I sleep better if I were loved?

SHE sits up.

That's not my name. My name is Spider, and I eat onions at the bottom of the sea.

EVKA

I have brought you an egg.

MILENA

Where are my books?

> *MILENA looks around. EVKA removes an egg from her*
> *apron pocket and holds it out toward Milena.*

EVKA

It's hard-boiled.

MILENA

I hate eggs. Bring me a pen. It's time to write my poem.

EVKA

You cannot eat poems. Eat your egg.

MILENA

I never eat before I swim. Poetry in the morning; swimming in the
afternoon.

EVKA

You need protein. You are pregnant.

> *EVKA peels the egg. The bits of shell fall to the floor.*

MILENA

Don't be ridiculous.

> *The ropes tug. MILENA stands up. SHE looks down.*
> *SHE is very pregnant.*

My god, I'm a balloon.

EVKA

Looks like triplets. Who are their fathers?

MILENA

I'll never fit into my swimsuit.

> *EVKA holds the egg out toward Milena. One of Milena's arms is lifted to egg-level. MILENA accepts the egg.*

EVKA

I've peeled it for you.

MILENA

Do you have salt?

EVKA

Of course.

> *EVKA removes a salt shaker from her apron, salts the egg for Milena, and returns the shaker to her apron.*

MILENA

Do you have ketchup?

EVKA

Yes.

> *EVKA removes a bottle of ketchup from her apron, uncaps it, pours ketchup on the egg, recaps and returns the bottle to her apron. MILENA nibbles the egg.*

MILENA

Do you have a safety pin?

> *SHE rummages through her apron.*

EVKA

I am prepared for every contingency. Rubber duck, teething ring, pacifier . . . safety pin.

SHE hands a giant safety pin to MILENA, who speedily unfastens it and aims as if to pierce her belly.

Red light!

Milena's arms are suddenly lifted above her head, and SHE drops the pin and the egg on the floor. EVKA retrieves the pin, fastens it, and stashes it in her apron.

MILENA

I'd so hoped to deflate.

EVKA

Think of the boys.

MILENA

What boys?

EVKA

The triplets.

MILENA

All boys? But I wanted a girl.

EVKA

You already have a girl.

The ropes slacken, and Milena's arms fall to her sides as OLINKA descends from above and dangles in the air directly above the cauldron.

OLINKA

Mama! Take me to the park, Mama! I want to ride the swing. I want a big red lollipop. I want cotton candy. I want a puppy. I want a pony. Please Mama can I please have a pony please please please?

MILENA

My daughter's a puppet?

EVKA

Naturally. But we need boys.

MILENA

I don't.

OLINKA

We need boys! We need toys!

EVKA

You make too much noise, Olinka.

OLINKA

Sorry.

MILENA

Please take her to the park. I want to write my poem.

EVKA

You're her mother.

MILENA

And you're my mother?

EVKA

Who told you that?

OLINKA

Mama! Mama! Watch me dance. I can dance!

OLINKA kicks her legs in the air.

EVKA

Good girl, Olinka! You've mastered a useful skill. Now you can dance in the parade.

OLINKA

Olé!

> *SHE curtsies.*

MILENA

I'm sorry. You must go. Back where you came from.

> *MILENA pulls Olinka's body as if it were a window shade, and suddenly Olinka is yanked up offstage.*

OLINKA

> *(As she exits.)*

Maamaaaa!

EVKA

That's no way to treat your daughter.

MILENA

She's not my daughter. I don't remember her.

EVKA

Do you remember yesterday?

MILENA

Yesterday: I awoke to my silent room and took my crisp black pen to a clean white page. I stretched my arms in the air, wiggled my fingers, and jotted down phrases inspired by my mustard-seed dreams and deepwater disposition. I wrote of dragonflies reverting to larvae, of a starfish with three pointed legs, of a giant squid that lost its shell. I contemplated a tuskless walrus and a finless shark. Then I hiked to the lake and swam mindless laps until my head was clear and my heart was calm, and I floated in the sun.

EVKA

What else?

MILENA

What do you mean?

EVKA

What else happened yesterday? Our capital was invaded. Our nation's at war.

MILENA

Why do you think the squid was shell-less?

EVKA

Since then, your life has changed.

MILENA

You mean these strings? They scratch.

EVKA

And your pregnancy?

MILENA

It bloats.

EVKA

And my presence?

MILENA

Worst of all. I want my quiet back. And my books: the ones with my name on the spine and the ones I've collected and treasured.

EVKA

You've already read them.

MILENA

I might read them again.

> *EVKA turns and exits. MILENA takes a few steps around the stage, basking in her freedom, until she finds herself restricted by the ropes. SHE pulls her arms and legs to the limits and finally slides to the ground and sits, defeated. EVKA returns with a stack of white paper, a white feather pen, and a jar of red ink.*

EVKA

For you, Milena.

> *EVKA hands the paper, pen, and ink to Milena. MILENA sets the items on the floor around her, opens the jar of ink, and dips her pen.*

MILENA

Now I can write my poem. My name is Spider, and I eat onions—

EVKA

No.

> *MILENA begins to write on the page. Suddenly, her arms are jerked back by the ropes, and the pen falls to the ground, splashing ink.*

MILENA

No!

> *MILENA tries to break free of the ropes and finally settles for retrieving the pen. SHE tries again.*

My name is—

> *Again the ropes pull her back, but this time they hold her arms high in the air.*

Let me go! Please. Let me go.

> *The ropes relax, dropping Milena's arms to her sides.*

Thank you. Am I free?

> *SHE cautiously rises, takes a few steps, and reaches the limits of the ropes.*

No.

EVKA bends down, scoops up a piece of paper stained with ink, and tears it to pieces.

Why bring me paper if you won't let me write?

EVKA

We need pamphlets. We're at war. This is no time for applesauce.

MILENA

Applesauce?

EVKA

If you write nonsense, no one will remember you when you're dead.

MILENA

You think I'll leave a legacy with propaganda?

EVKA

If you had your life to do over again, Milena, would you undo your mistakes?

MILENA

My mistakes? . . . Once, when I was a girl, down by the river, under a bridge, three boys cut the fins off a fish and tossed it back in the water just to see it bleed and die. I'd like to undo that.

EVKA

You should have hit its head with a rock and brought it home to mother.

MILENA

I wanted it to swim off and live happily ever after. Instead I watched it suffer.

EVKA

You think like a child. Consider the future.

MILENA

What future?

EVKA

Think of your boys.

MILENA

Those unborn, ill-conceived triplets you've somehow saddled me with? They'll be fish-killers, too; I can tell from their kicks. I don't want to be their mother.

OLINKA descends, wearing a diving mask and holding a rubber fish.

OLINKA

Mama! Mama! I've been swimming.

EVKA

Olinka, you were supposed to practice cooking, sewing, and marching.

OLINKA

Watch me swim, Mama!

OLINKA wades through the air, the lights dim, and a school of fish is projected on the wall. OLINKA stops, the lights come up, and the projections vanish.

MILENA

Good girl, Olinka! You've mastered a useful skill. Would you like to write a poem?

OLINKA

I have a pet fish. His name is Rover.

EVKA

We'll cook that fish for dinner.

EVKA grabs the fish from Olinka.

OLINKA

Nooooooooooooooooooo!

MILENA

We're having duck for dinner.

EVKA

You're in no position to make decisions.

> *Milena's arms and legs are pulled in random directions by the ropes.*

MILENA

All right! That hurts! Please stop. I'll write your propaganda for you.

> *The ropes slacken.*

A call to arms. And legs. . . . And fish.

EVKA

You must take your mission seriously. I tell you for your own good. Your good is the good of the nation.

MILENA

If you say so.

> *The ropes tug at Milena.*

I said I'd do it.

> *The ropes slacken.*

EVKA

You must believe in the cause.

MILENA

I believe in the cause.

EVKA

Sincerely.

MILENA

I believe in the cause. Sincerely. I promise. Watch.

> *MILENA sits on the floor, dips the pen in ink, and is about to scrawl on the paper when suddenly, instead of writing, she pierces her balloon belly with the inky nib. Her belly pops and deflates.*

OLINKA

Maamaaaaaaaaaaaaaaaaaaaaaaaaaaaa!

MILENA

Don't worry, Olinka. I wanted a girl.

EVKA

Useless. Useless. I don't know why I bother. I'm not your mother!

> *EVKA storms off, tossing the fish into the fray. As she exits, Milena's ropes start pooling on the ground around her.*

MILENA

(*To Olinka.*)
No more scratchy strings.

> *MILENA slides the ropes off her wrists.*

You too, my daughter. You can write your poem, too.

> *MILENA slashes Olinka's strings with her pen, and OLINKA drops into the cauldron. MILENA doesn't notice.*

We're free, my darling. Free.

> *MILENA sits on the ground among her papers, the scattered egg, the rubber fish.*

Poetry in the morning. Swimming in the afternoon.

SHE picks up the pen and begins to write.

My name is Spider,
and I eat onions at the bottom of the sea.

END OF SCENE 3

TRANSITION

MILENA transforms into Witch 1 as WITCHES 2 AND 3 appear. The WITCHES sweep up the mess and push the cauldron back to the center of the stage as they chant:

Anna Marvanová, born 1928.
Her voice vanished from Prague, 1969.

Jana Sternová, born 1921.
Her dance vanished from Prague, 1969.

Eva Kantůrková, born 1930.
Her words vanished from Prague, 1970.

Marta Kubišová, born 1942.
Her music vanished from Prague, 1970.

WITCH 2 takes a factory worker's smock from the cauldron and puts it on. SHE takes a pair of red, high-heeled shoes from the cauldron, examines them with delight, and steps into them as she becomes Angélica. WITCH 1 starts to exit. WITCH 3 blocks her, lights a cigarette, and hands it to Witch 1.

SCENE 4

LA CENICIENTA (PART 2)

The shoe's just right, and there's no blood at all.
She's truly the bride you met at the ball.

—The Brothers Grimm

CHARACTERS

WITCH 1, WITCH 3   *Cocktail dresses.*
ANGÉLICA   *12. SHE wears a factory worker's*
                                   smock and an extremely high-heeled
                                   pair of red shoes—shoes that a
                                   12-year-old girl might find attractive.

SETTING

A circle of eyeless rag dolls hangs above the cauldron (center).

AT RISE

WITCH 1 leans against the cauldron and smokes a cigarette. ANGÉLICA
addresses Witch 1.

ANGÉLICA

In Durango, it's all donkeys and dirt. There's nothing to do there, and everyone is boring. Do you know it took 12 hours to get here by bus? And I am 12 years old. And I made 21 dollars last week, which is 12 backwards. So 12's my lucky number. But don't tell anyone because you have to be 16 to work in the *maquiladora*.

Suddenly, a whistle blows and the dolls start to revolve. WITCH 1 tosses her cigarette into the cauldron, pulls out a glue gun, and, as each doll passes, SHE shoots the spot where its eyes should be. The sounds of a factory accompany her movements.

I have a fake ID that says I'm 16. Mamá and Papá spent their savings to buy it for me, so I have to send them money in Durango. But I also get to buy shoes!

WITCH 3 enters and blows a whistle. The dolls stop revolving, WITCH 1 stops working, and the factory sounds cease, but ANGÉLICA keeps talking.

I used my first week's pay to buy these. They make me so tall I can look down at the world. I bet Mamá never had shoes like these. She didn't want to send me away, but they need money for medicine, plus there wasn't anything for me to do there. Here I can go dancing!

WITCH 3 blows the whistle until finally ANGÉLICA stops speaking.

What? I thought it was break.

WITCH 3

Break's over. You're a disruptive personality, López, slowing down the line, slowing down your team. There've been complaints.

WITCH 1 glowers.

ANGÉLICA

I am a fast worker. I have little fingers, just the right size to handle these tiny eyes.

SHE holds up a handful of black buttons and accidentally spills them on the floor.

Oh no!

SHE tries to pick up the buttons but trips because of her shoes. SHE lands on the ground.

WITCH 3

That's it, López. You're fired.

ANGÉLICA

Fired?

WITCH 3

Go on. Clean out your locker and get out of here.

ANGÉLICA

Right now? But it's the middle of the night. I haven't finished my shift. And there aren't any buses.

WITCH 3

Now.

ANGÉLICA

And my feet hurt.

WITCH 3

You don't work here anymore, López. Get out. You're trespassing. I'll have you physically removed

ANGÉLICA

But it's still dark.

WITCH 1

What's the matter, Angélica? You afraid?

ANGÉLICA

Of course not.

WITCH 1

Well you should be. Haven't you heard? Girls are disappearing in Juárez.

WITCH 3 blows her whistle. ANGÉLICA gets up and exits quickly. The dolls revolve. Factory noises resume. Lights down. WITCH 3 cackles. The dolls drop into the pot.

END OF SCENE 4

TRANSITION

The WITCHES chant:

Miriam Cristina Gallegos, age 17.
Vanished from Juárez, Mexico. May 4, 2000.

Maria de los Angeles Acosta, age 19.
Vanished from Juárez, Mexico. April 25, 2001.

Guadalupe Luna de la Rosa, age 19.
Vanished from Juárez, Mexico. September 30, 2001.

Alma M. Lopez Garza, age 27.
Vanished from Juárez, Mexico. February 25, 2002.

Rosa M. Mayela Ituarte Silva, age 37.
Vanished from Juárez, Mexico. November 21, 2002.

Luisa Garcia Hernandez, age 14.
Vanished from Juárez, Mexico. January 20, 2003.

Ana Laura Garcia Castrejon, age 24.
Vanished from Juárez, Mexico. July 21, 2004.

Julia Hernandez Hernandez, age 20.
Vanished from Juárez, Mexico. August 11, 2004.

Edith Aranda Longorio, age 22.
Vanished from Juárez, Mexico. May 3, 2005.

Irma Elizabeth Vargas, age 16.
Vanished from Juárez, Mexico. August 4, 2005.

Lupita Perez Montes, age 17.
Vanished from Juárez, Mexico. January 31, 2009.

Monica Janeth Alanis, age 18.
Vanished from Juárez, Mexico. March 26, 2009.

WITCHES 2 AND 3 vanish. WITCH 1 takes a pair of geeky glasses and a book from the cauldron. SHE puts on the glasses and opens the book.

SCENE 5

LUPUS

Children, especially attractive, well bred young ladies, should never talk to strangers, for if they should do so, they may well provide dinner for a wolf.

—Charles Perrault

CHARACTERS

RED	*Red hood, cocktail dress.*
WOLF	*Wolf mask, cocktail dress.*
WITCH 1	*Cocktail dress.*

SETTING

The cauldron (center).

AT RISE

WITCH 1 wears geeky glasses and holds an open book, from which SHE reads to the audience.

WITCH 1

Once there was a girl whose mother died. Her father remarried, and her stepmother and stepsisters were very mean. They made her do chores while they went dancing.

> *RED enters, skipping. SHE carries a basket. WITCH 1 looks at her with disdain.*

Wrong story.

RED

> I'm on my way to Grandmother's house.

WITCH 1

> You're supposed to be Aschenputtel.

RED

>> *(Louder.)*
>
> I'm on my way to Grandmother's house.

>> *WITCH 1 gives in and turns the pages until she finds another story. SHE reads to the audience.*

WITCH 1

> Once there was a girl whose mother sent her across the forest with a basket of goodies for Grandmother. The mother warned her to stay on the path, but the girl decided to pick some berries.

>> *RED plops herself down on the edge of the cauldron and takes a toy kaleidoscope from the basket. SHE looks up at the sky as if through a telescope.*

> I said, "but the girl decided to pick some berries."

RED

> It's almost twilight. What a perfect time to study my astronomy.

WITCH 1

> While the girl was distracted, a wolf snuck up on her. It had great big fangs.

>> *As RED gazes up through her kaleidoscope, WOLF enters riding a little girl's bicycle, ringing its bell. SHE stops in front of Red.*

WOLF

> Hello, little girl. What are you doing here in the woods all alone at twilight?

RED

> *(Still gazing at the sky.)*
> I'm looking for a comet.

WOLF

> A what?

RED

> A cosmic snowball of frozen gas.

WOLF

> That's something you don't see every day.

RED

> You have to know what to look for. Comets have fiery tails and . . .

WOLF

> Tall pointy ears? Great big fangs?

RED

> *(Finally looking at Wolf.)*
> Who are you?

WOLF

> My name is Lupita.

RED

> Lupita? That's funny. I was just observing the constellation Lupus. It's my favorite constellation. It looks like a wolf. Actually, so do you.

WOLF

> May I see?

RED

> Sure.

> > *WOLF dismounts from the bicycle and leans it against the cauldron. SHE sits beside Red, and RED hands her the kaleidoscope.*

WOLF

> Wow. This is so cool.

WITCH 1

> The wolf wanted to devour the little girl, so she devised a plan to trick her. She asked the little girl . . .

> *Silence.*

> I said: She asked the little girl . . .

WOLF

> *(Staring at the stars.)*
> Um . . . little girl . . . um . . . what are you doing here in the woods all alone at twilight?

RED

> I'm on my way to Grandmother's house. My mother sent me to bring her some cake and a pot of butter, and we're going to have a slumber party.

WOLF

> You have a grandmother?

RED

> Sure. Don't you?

WOLF

> I don't even have a mother. I'm an orphan. I'm from an endangered species.

RED

> Oh, I'm sorry. That's very sad. Would you like to come to Grandmother's house and join our slumber party?

WOLF

> Sure. That sounds like fun. Hey look! Over there!

RED

>What?

WOLF

>I think it's a comet.

>>*WOLF hands Red the kaleidoscope.*

RED

>A comet!

>>*WOLF and RED stare at the sky in wonder. WITCH 1 looks, too. Silence as the comet passes.*

WOLF

>That was so cool!

RED

>What great eyes you have, Lupita.

WOLF

>Now show me Lupus.

>>*RED adjusts the kaleidoscope and hands it back to Wolf.*

RED

>>*(Pointing.)*
>There.

WITCH 1

>>*(Clearing her throat.)*
>The wolf wanted to devour the little girl.

WOLF

>>*(To Witch 1.)*
>Didn't you hear what she said? These stars are named for *me*.

RED

> We need to get to Grandmother's before dark. It takes a while to walk there.

WITCH 1

> The wolf suggested they race to Grandmother's house.

WOLF

> *(To Witch 1.)*
> I'm thinking of becoming a vegan.

WITCH 1

> The *hungry* wolf knew that she could get there first, and that way she could eat both the girl and the grandmother for dinner. *Mm, mm good.*

RED

> Let's go.

> *RED is about to get up, but WOLF stops her.*

WOLF

> Don't worry. We can ride together on my bike. But first: Can you show me more constellations?

RED

> Okay. Look up there.

> *RED points to the sky.*

> That one's Andromeda.

WOLF

> Andromeda?

RED

> Her parents tied her to a rock so a sea monster could eat her, but in the end, she escaped.

WOLF

How'd she do that?

RED

In one popular version of the story, after the sea monster devoured her and her grandmother, a huntsman came along and slit open the sea monster's belly, thereby freeing Andromeda and her grandmother.

WOLF

What happened to the sea monster?

RED

It was dead.

WOLF

Oh.

RED

And the world was safe for little girls.

WOLF

Oh. I was hoping for a happy ending.

RED

That is a happy ending!

WOLF

Not for the sea monster.

RED

The sea monster is the bad guy. He's not supposed to have a happy ending.

WOLF

I feel bad for him.

RED

You can't feel bad for bad guys. If you do, the world will just walk all over you. That's what Grandmother says.

WOLF

> I'm getting hungry.

RED

> Let's go. We can roast marshmallows when we get there.

WOLF

> Very hungry. I was hoping for something more substantial.

RED

> We can order pizza.

WOLF

> Meat-lovers' special?

RED

> With extra cheese!

WOLF

> Then we'll live happily ever after.

RED

> Right on!

> > *WOLF and RED hop down from the cauldron, get on the bicycle, and ride away, ringing the bell.*

> > *WITCH 1 slams her book shut.*

WITCH 1
> The end.

> > *Silence. Then . . . offstage—a blood-curdling scream. WITCH 1 vanishes.*

END OF SCENE 5

TRANSITION

The WITCHES appear.

WITCH 1

Fair is foul.

WITCH 3

And foul is fair.

WITCH 2

Hover through the fog and filthy air.

> *A rag doll dangles above the cauldron. The WITCHES hang red velvet curtains in front of the cauldron. WITCH 3 opens and closes the curtains to make sure they work. As THEY set up the scene, the WITCHES chant.*

Maria Luisa Vega.
Vanished from Argentina. 1975.

Adela Carmen Mercado.
Vanished from Argentina. 1975.

Gladys Lucia Gomez.
Vanished from Argentina. 1975.

Maria Inés del Carmen Atim.
Vanished from Argentina. 1975.

Graciela Maorenzic.
Vanished from Argentina. 1975.

Elsa Gider de Kroyem.
Vanished from Argentina. 1975.

Marta Graciela Acuña.
Vanished from Argentina. 1975.

Amalaia Moavro de Patiño, three months pregnant.
Vanished from Argentina. 1975.

The doll falls into the pot. The WITCHES vanish.

SCENE 6

THIS OLIVE GREW IN EDEN

Inspired by the story of Inés of Herrera del Duque, the Prophetess of Extremadura (1488-1500).

CHARACTERS

INÉS   *A prophetess. 11. Wears white.*
                              Holds a staff like a shepherdess.
BEATRIZ   *A cousin of Inés. 13. Wears white.*
ISABEL (et al.)   *A cousin of Inés and, gradually, a*
                              crowd of girls just like her. 17+. A
                              single puppet that begins as one
                              teenaged girl and grows into nine—a
                              body with nine heads. The heads are
                              human. The body is that of a sheep.

SETTING

An old-fashioned puppet theater (the cauldron) sits center stage.

AT RISE

The puppet-theater curtains are closed. ISABEL (one head) appears in front of the closed curtains and addresses the audience. SHE wears a red cross.

ISABEL
    In fourteen hundred ninety-two
    Columbus sailed the ocean blue.
    The king and queen of sunny Spain
    Supplied his ships and hoped for gain.
    Meanwhile in their local news

Ferdinand and Isabella told the Jews
You must convert and be good Catholics,
Or we will kill you. Take your pick.
Many Jews fled across Spain's borders
After hearing the Inquisition's orders.
Those who stayed behind converted
And they had their freedoms thwarted.
This is the story of some converted girls,
Who grew up in this hostile world.

> *ISABEL exits. The curtains part to reveal the heads, arms, and torsos of Beatriz and Inés. (Perhaps their legs are in the cauldron.)*

BEATRIZ

My neck hurts.

INÉS

That's nothing.

BEATRIZ

I know. But can't we lie on our backs?

> *BEATRIZ attempts to recline, but INÉS nudges her with her staff.*

INÉS

No. We might fall asleep.

BEATRIZ

I'm hungry.

INÉS

That's nothing. Don't you want to see your mother?

> *ISABEL enters and hovers before the puppet theater.*

ISABEL

> Inés! Beatriz! It's time for dinner. Come along, cousins. Come wash your hands. It's time to say grace.

INÉS

> We're fasting. We can't eat till we see the stars.

BEATRIZ

> And we don't say grace. We say *ha-motzi.*

ISABEL

> You say what?

INÉS

> *Ha-motzi.*

ISABEL

> Are you insane? Where did you hear about *ha-motzi?*

INÉS

> From my mother.

ISABEL

> Your mother died when you were two.

INÉS

> I saw her yesterday.

ISABEL

> In a dream.

INÉS

> It felt like a dream, but I know it was real because when I awoke, I still had this.

> *INÉS holds up an olive.*

This olive grew in Eden.

> *ISABEL grabs the olive with her teeth and eats it.*

ISABEL

You mustn't say such things. They'll hear you.

INÉS

I speak the truth. I hope they hear me.

> *SHE raises her staff and sings in Hebrew.*

L'shana habaah b'yerushalayim . . .

ISABEL

That was her song.

> *ISABEL exits.*

BEATRIZ

Now you've done it.

INÉS

That's nothing.

> *INÉS and BEATRIZ continue to gaze at the sky. Darkness. Stars. Time passes (quickly): Soft music plays as the stars orbit Inés and Beatriz. Lights up. ISABEL (et al.) enters and hovers before the puppet theater. SHE now has three heads.*

ISABEL (et al.)

Inés! I've brought friends.

BEATRIZ

Have you brought food?

An apple descends from above and dangles before the puppet theater. INÉS and BEATRIZ stop staring at the sky as they watch it hang there. BEATRIZ takes the apple and is about to bite it, but instead SHE holds it out to Inés.

INÉS

No thank you. I don't get hungry anymore. Just don't forget to say the *brochah.*

BEATRIZ mumbles a blessing and bites the apple.

ISABEL (et al.)
The *brochah!* You'll get us all killed.

BEATRIZ
She'll get us all saved. But we'll have to stay awake to see it.

ISABEL (et al.)
Saved? We'll be burned at the stake.

INÉS

The prophet Elias will announce our redemption on March eighth.

BEATRIZ

Then an Angel will lead us to the Promised Land—where there'll be cake and cookies for us to eat, and spotted horses for us to ride, and silky dresses for us to wear, and cute boys for us to marry. Thus spake the prophetess Inés.

INÉS

Thus spake my Heavenly mother. With embellishments from Beatriz.

ISABEL (et al.)
Boys?

BEATRIZ
Cute boys.

ISABEL (et al.)
Boys!

ISABEL (et al.)'s heads baa and bob.

INÉS

She did not say "cute." She said "studious and faithful" and that our fathers will approve. She said we will live spiritually and shamelessly, in solidarity, in a land of bread and fruit, like frolicking lambs in a field of plenty.

ISABEL (et al.)
You're ten years old.

INÉS

Eleven.

ISABEL (et al.)
Why should we believe you?

ISABEL (et al.)'s heads baa and bob.

INÉS

Because you want to. We have five months. We must prepare. We must be pure. The Angel will appear on a Monday and then take us from here four days later. We must be clean. We must wear white. We must leave behind our jewels and cross a river. For more instructions, read this letter.

A blank piece of white paper descends from above and dangles before the puppet theater.

This missive came from Heaven. I am its messenger.

ISABEL (et al.) grabs the letter and studies it.

ISABEL (et al.)
There's nothing written.

INÉS

>You'll see the writing when you're ready.
>   *(Singing in Hebrew.)*
>L'shana habaah b'yerushalayim . . .

>>*ISABEL (et al.) exits. INÉS and BEATRIZ resume their sky vigil. Darkness. Stars. BEATRIZ sleeps. Time passes (quickly): Soft music plays as the stars orbit Inés and Beatriz. Lights up. BEATRIZ awakens. ISABEL (et al.) enters and hovers before the puppet theater. SHE has nine heads.*

ISABEL (et al.)

>Inés! We've come for more predictions. We've cleansed ourselves and dressed in white. We'll wait with you for Heaven, stare with you at the stars, Inés.

INÉS

>My mother named me Ester.

ISABEL (et al.)

>When did you last see her?

INÉS

>This afternoon.

>>*INÉS rises and addresses ISABEL (et al.) and BEATRIZ as if delivering a sermon.*

I saw the stars at daytime. Polaris shined at noon, then the Dog Star, and then I saw my mother. The star that is my mother shines with a subtle fire.

She drew me up to Heaven, where I soared into Eden. She led me with her saffron glow through its sapphire-spangled gates. She fed me figs and grapes and pomegranates. She wore silk and feathers, and cradled me in her soft embrace. When she released me, I floated among the stars at peace.

(To Beatriz.)

I saw your mother, too. She said she misses you.

> *A white carnation descends from above and dangles before*
> *the puppet theater. INÉS takes it and hands it to Beatriz.*

This flower bloomed in Eden.

ISABEL (et al.)

A celestial carnation!

> *ISABEL (et al.)'s heads baa and bob.*

BEATRIZ

(To Inés.)

But you promised to take me this time.

INÉS

(To Beatriz.)

You shouldn't have fallen asleep.

BEATRIZ

(To Inés.)

You promised to take me to Heaven.

ISABEL (et al.)

Oh, Inés, you've been to Heaven. We want to go there, too.

INÉS

The prophet Elias will announce our redemption. Then an Angel will lead us to the Promised Land.

BEATRIZ

(To Inés.)

Is that a promise, too?

ISABEL (et al.)

Just one thing, Inés. Can you tell them to hurry?

INÉS

They will arrive on March eighth.

ISABEL (et al.)

That's two months. That's too long.

INÉS

The stars move slowly.

ISABEL (et al.)

We're afraid for our lives.

BEATRIZ

So am I.

INÉS

That's nothing.

BEATRIZ

Everything's nothing to you.

> *ISABEL (et al.) exits. Darkness. Stars. BEATRIZ climbs out of the cauldron and tiptoes away. Time passes (quickly): Soft music plays as the stars orbit Inés. Lights up. ISABEL (et al.) enters and hovers before the puppet theater. She has five heads.*

ISABEL (et al.)

Inés! They've christened you a zealot. They claim you're a heretic. You must run.

INÉS

Where's Beatriz?

ISABEL (et al.)

She's confessed.

INÉS

To what? Beatriz is chaste and blameless.

ISABEL (et al.)

She saved herself by damning you.

INÉS

My cousin.

ISABEL (et al.)

If they arrest us, we'll be forced to confess too. You must hide. Take cover. This hilltop's so exposed.

INÉS

We must await the Angel.

ISABEL (et al.)

They've begun their executions. Notice our numbers are dwindling.

ISABEL (et al.)'s heads baa and bob.

INÉS

My star will guard our safety.

ISABEL (et al.)

That's not enough.

INÉS

The Messiah's on his way.

ISABEL (et al.)

So is the Inquisition.

ISABEL (et al.) exits. INÉS stands and stares up at the sky. Darkness. Stars. Time passes (quickly): Soft music plays as the stars orbit Inés. Lights up. A sound in the distance.

INÉS

    Mother?

            Twilight. Another sound.

    Mother, is that you?

BEATRIZ (offstage)

    Of course it's me.

            The sound of footsteps approaching. BEATRIZ enters,
            unrecognizable in a hooded red robe and carrying a loop of
            rope. INÉS remains still, staring at the sky.

    It's me, darling Ester. I'll take you to Heaven.
        (Singing in Hebrew.)
    L'shana habaah b'yerushalayim . . .

            BEATRIZ takes Inés' staff and uses it to lead Inés out of
            the puppet theater. THEY stand before the open curtains.
            BEATRIZ plants the staff in the ground behind Inés and
            ties her to it.

BEATRIZ

    Don't move.

            BEATRIZ continues to stand behind Inés, flings off
            her hood, and stares ahead. Then, BEATRIZ lights a
            match. Total darkness.

INÉS

    That's nothing.

            Soft music plays. Lights up. BEATRIZ and INÉS have
            vanished. The puppet theater curtains are drawn. In front
            of it, a stake smolders. ISABEL pokes one head out from
            between the curtains.

ISABEL
    Inés!

          SHE looks at the stake with fear, and vanishes.

END OF SCENE 6

TRANSITION

The WITCHES appear and dismantle the puppet theater as they chant:

ALL

Helen Claire Frost, age 17.
Last seen leaving her apartment in Prince George, British Columbia, near Highway 16. 1970.

Virginia Sampare, age 18.
Vanished at Gitsegukla, British Columbia, along Highway 16. 1971.

Shelly-Ann Bacsu, age 16.
Vanished near Hinton, Alberta, walking home along Highway 16. 1983.

Cecilia Anne Nikal, age unknown.
Last seen in Smithers, British Columbia, on Highway 16. 1989.

Delphine Nikal, age 16.
Vanished from Smithers, British Columbia, hitchhiking east on Highway 16. 1995.

Nicole Hoar, age 25.
Vanished while hitchhiking to Smithers, British Columbia, on Highway 16. 2002.

Margaret Nooski, age 89.
Vanished from Fraser Lake, British Columbia, hitchhiking on the Nautley Road turnoff on Highway 16. 2004.

Tamara Chipman, age 22.
Vanished from Prince Rupert, British Columbia, hitchhiking east on Highway 16. 2005.

WITCHES 1 AND 2 vanish. WITCH 3 takes a pair of geeky glasses and a book from the cauldron. She puts on the glasses and opens the book.

SCENE 7

AIMÉE

In her obscurity, in her inaccessibility, in her very imprisonment, lay her strength.

—Richard Halliburton, *Seven League Boots*

CHARACTERS

WITCH 1, WITCH 3   *Cocktail dresses.*
AIMÉE   *A little girl's dress.*

SETTING

The cauldron (center).

AT RISE

One rag doll hangs above the cauldron, staring motionless ahead. WITCH 3 wears geeky glasses and holds an open book, from which SHE reads to the audience.

WITCH 3
Once upon a time, a long long time ago and far far away, lived a little girl who got lost at sea.

> *AIMÉE enters. SHE stands center stage and gazes out on the horizon, as if standing on the deck of a ship.*

Her name was Aimée—Aimée du Buc de Rivéry—and while her family lived in Martinique, she was sent to France for school. She was a cousin of Josephine, Napoleon's wife. She lived in the late eighteenth century. This much is fact.

WITCH 3 looks up from the book and addresses the audience.

What happened next is legend. On her way home from France, her ship vanished. Of course there might have just been a bad storm.

Thunder. Lightning. AIMÉE cowers.

But most agree that pirates raided the ship. Barbary pirates. And took Aimée away.

WITCH 1 enters wearing a black eye patch.

WITCH 1
Yarrr!

WITCH 1 grabs Aimée and drags her offstage.

WITCH 3
And then, who knows? Except some say they sold her to the Ottoman sultan . . .

AIMÉE re-enters wearing her cocktail dress and a veil.

. . . and she grew up among his harem . . .

Harem music plays, and AIMÉE does a belly dance.

. . . and made a lot of friends.

WITCH 1 enters, also wearing a veil, and joins in the dance.

Because of her Frenchness, everyone admired her.

The music and dancing stop. WITCH 1 looks charmed by Aimée.

She was consulted for all kinds of advice, including decorating . . .

> *AIMÉE points at the cauldron and indicates a better place for it. WITCH 1 pushes it two inches in that direction, as if with all her might.*

And foreign affairs.

> *AIMÉE points at the cauldron. WITCH 1 reaches inside it and pulls out a saber. SHE poses as if ready to mutilate someone. AIMÉE shakes her head, bored. WITCH 1 tosses the saber into the cauldron and pulls out a white carnation. SHE poses as if about to present it. AIMÉE nods with approval and accepts the carnation.*

She was of course the sultan's favorite, and she bore his eldest son.

> *WITCH 1 removes a swaddled bundle from the cauldron and hands it to AIMÉE, who drops the carnation and holds the bundle as if it were a baby.*

Which means she became the mother of a sultan. And lived happily ever after.

> *WITCH 3 slams the book shut and tosses it into the cauldron. AIMÉE dances happily away, clutching the baby. WITCH 1 exits behind her, grabbing the carnation off the floor.*

Of course if you dig too deep, you'll find complications.

Some say Aimée was nine years old when she vanished; some say 18. Some say two. Some say she was the mother of Mahmud II, but Mahmud II was born six years before Aimée boarded that ship.

From an imperialist perspective, this fairy tale explains how a woman could have had as much influence as this sultan's mother supposedly had: She was Western.

In its many incarnations, it explains the bond between France and the Ottoman Empire. More recently that story's been spun as anti-Islamic backlash, with Aimée the victim of a misogynist regime.

Just think of how many books this missing girl has sold.

If only she'd survived, she'd never have been anyone.

The doll falls into the pot.

END OF SCENE 7

TRANSITION

The WITCHES link hands and dance.

ALL

    The weïrd sisters, hand in hand,
    Posters of the sea and land,
    Thus do go, about, about:
    Thrice to thine and thrice to mine
    And thrice again, to make up nine.

THEY stop dancing.

WITCH 3

    Where next, sisters?

WITCH 2

    Who knows?

WITCH 1

    The earth hath bubbles, as the water has.

WITCH 2

    And we are of them.

A seagull squawks. WITCH 3 removes some rags from the cauldron and wraps them around her feet. WITCHES 1 AND 2 push the cauldron to a corner. THEY take red flags from the cauldron and plant them in four corners to demarcate a square. One corner is the cauldron, with a flag now rising from its center. WITCH 3 lies down and transforms into Sveta. A pile of white feathers rains down on her. As the WITCHES perform these actions, THEY chant:

ALL

Joanne Ratcliffe, age 11, and Kirsty Gordon, age 4.
Vanished from Adelaide Oval, South Australia. 1973.

Eloise Worledge, age 8.
Vanished from her bedroom in Beaumaris, Victoria, Austrialia. 1976.

Azaria Chamberlain, nine weeks old.
Vanished from Uluru, Australia. 1980.

Charmian Faulkner, age 2.
Vanished from St. Kilda, Melbourne, Australia. 1980.

> *WITCHES 1 AND 2 vanish. A seagull soars in, squawks, and lands atop the feathers.*

SCENE 8

KILOMETER 14

"You know," whispered the woman next to me through chattering teeth, cowering as low as possible against the wind, "it wouldn't surprise me in the least if a mammoth came out from behind that hill." I agreed with her. I too felt that we were getting farther and farther away, not only from towns but from the present era, toward the Neolithic age.

—Eugenia Semyonovna Ginzburg, *Journey into the Whirlwind*

CHARACTERS

MANYA	*SHE wears colorless, tattered rags and too-big red boots.*
SVETA	*SHE wears colorless, tattered rags. Instead of shoes, SHE's wrapped rags around her feet.*
MAMMOTH	*A mammoth. Red.*

SETTING

A pile of white feathers dominates a very white stage. A seagull sleeps on the feathers. Four red flags demarcate a square space that surrounds the feathers. In a corner, the cauldron; one of the flags rises from its center.

AT RISE

Silence. Then: The seagull awakens, squawks, and flies away. Suddenly, the stack of feathers erupts as SVETA, who's been buried inside it, rises. SHE looks around, picks a feather off her clothing, and brushes it on her cheek.

SVETA

Am I a baby snow goose, newly hatched with downy feathers?

Apparently not since I see no shell.
I could be a polar bear.

> *SHE inspects her hands for claws.*

A long-horned goat.

> *SHE inspects her head for horns.*

A tiger.

> *SHE roars.*

I'd rather be a mammoth.

> *Silence. Then: The sound of footsteps approaching. SVETA looks for a place to hide, but she can't cross the flagged boundary. MANYA enters.*

Manya! I thought you were a mammoth. Clomping. How did you get out?

MANYA

I found boots.

> *SVETA and MANYA stare at Manya's feet. Her boots are enormous.*

SVETA

Were they attached to feet?

MANYA

Help me pull them off. They're for you.

SVETA

I don't need them. I'm not cold anymore. I've decided the snowflakes are feathers.

MANYA

> I admire your imagination.

SVETA

> You do? I've decided I'm a duckling. Look: webbed feet.

> *SVETA lifts a foot toward Manya.*

MANYA

> I admire your ability to adapt.

SVETA

> Since when?

> *MANYA sits on the ground and puts her feet in the air.*

> I said no thank you.

MANYA

> For the good of the party, comrade. Take them.

> *SVETA pulls the boots off Manya's feet and inspects them. MANYA continues to sit, her arms crossed in front of her.*

SVETA

> Fur. Leather.

> *SHE smells the boots.*

> Musk. Sweat.

MANYA

> Put them on your feet.

> *SVETA puts on the boots and waddles around, closely observing the boundaries created by the flags.*

SVETA

Where did you go? Why didn't they shoot you?

MANYA

You talk too much, comrade.

SVETA

When I was a girl, I had boots with fur lining. Rabbit white and soft, but heels like spikes. They hurt my feet.

MANYA

These don't?

SVETA

I can't feel my feet.

MANYA

That's good. You don't feel pain.

SVETA

Wouldn't you like to see a mammoth? One might suddenly appear: erupting from the ice or falling from the sky.

MANYA

Mammoths have been extinct in Eurasia since the beginning of the Holocene era. The last mammoths died on an arctic island, not far from here, 3,700 years ago. That's relatively recent, but not recent enough for us to see one.

SVETA

Just because no one's seen them doesn't mean they don't exist.

MANYA

I am a scientist. You are a philosopher.

SVETA

And we are both lumberjacks.

MANYA

But there aren't any trees. Yet they insist we meet quota.

SVETA

Or they'll shoot us.

MANYA

Or starve us. They won't give us soup.

SVETA

Soup! I used to love soup. Mushroom, onion, seafood. Borscht! I liked mine hot. What was your favorite?

MANYA

Mine? I don't remember. But Aleksei . . . Aleksei preferred cabbage. And the children loved chicken. I'd roast a whole bird for the broth— not boiled bones. I'd add carrots, parsnips, rutabagas. Oleg loved fat noodles. I'd warn him not to slurp. Maya loved potatoes. She'd chop them into mush. The potatoes . . . They'd frozen in the field.

SVETA

You've never mentioned your children.

MANYA

I need you to remember.

SVETA

That's easy: Oleg loved fat noodles. And Maya loved potatoes.

MANYA

They'll never find my grave.

SVETA

No one knows we're here. Even I don't know: Where's here?

MANYA

Kilometer 14.

SCENE 9

FOUR TIMES

I talked about my own life and about the girls imprisoned in brothels as slaves. I talked about how badly they are treated, the violence that they must endure. I talked about the gentle smile of Cambodian girls, and how that smile isn't genuine.

—Somaly Mam, *The Road of Lost Innocence*

CHARACTERS

CHANTHAVY (DOLL)	*A little girl, pristine and white; a bow on her head. Played by a china doll.*
CHANTHAVY (HUMAN)	*A little girl, filthy and feral. Same bow on her head.*
MOTHER	*Young and poor. She wears worn-out red flip-flops.*

SETTING

In a corner, the cauldron.

AT RISE

The cauldron in darkness. CHANTHAVY (DOLL) looms center stage (held by Witch 2). SHE holds a red helium balloon and addresses the audience.

CHANTHAVY (DOLL)
I was a virgin four times.
Each time they sewed me back together so I could bleed again.
Each time I cured a man of AIDS.
AIDS is a very bad disease, and the only cure is me.

They rented me by the week. A thousand dollars a week. For me!
Because I was a virgin, I was very valuable: I made men pure.
They knew I was a virgin because I was five years old.
They loved me. And I loved them too!
And they were very good to me, oh yes.
They called me pretty names.
I don't know what they mean, but they sounded so adult.
I love being an adult.
Lots of little girls pretend to be grown-up, but I really am.
I was lucky. I didn't have to wait till I was 12.
I didn't waste my best years. I didn't play with dolls.
I didn't play with girls. I didn't even play with boys.
I graduated right away. I got to play with men.
I loved it when they popped my cherry.

The balloon pops.

All four times.

Cherries rain from above. CHANTHAVY (DOLL) bows and descends to the floor as the lights dim on her. Lights up on the cauldron. CHANTHAVY (HUMAN) is tied to it like a dog to a tree; SHE even wears a collar. SHE growls, sniffs, and makes animal noises as SHE crawls around the stage. SHE finds the cherries and eats them, wildly, stuffing them into her mouth and smearing the red juice on her hands and clothes. SHE howls. A stained rag doll descends from above. CHANTHAVY (HUMAN) grabs it and seems like SHE is about to clutch it to her chest and hug it, but instead, SHE slams its head against the floor.

CHANTHAVY (HUMAN)
Cunt. Bitch. Whore. Ugly ugly ugly ugly worthless worthless worthless whore.

SHE slams the doll repeatedly, staining it with cherry juice.

What can you do, whore? Can you smile?

> *SHE uses her finger to paint a cherry-juice smile on the doll's face.*

Can you dance?

> *SHE makes the doll dance and lifts its skirt.*

Can you fuck?

> *SHE turns the doll upside down, letting its dress fall down over its legs, and tears the legs apart. Loud tearing noise.*

You like it. Say you like it. You know you like it. Now ask for more.

> *A lighter descends from above. SHE grabs it, lights it, and holds the flame between the doll's legs.*

Go on, ask me. Beg me.

> *A firecracker descends from above. SHE grabs the firecracker, lights it, and shoves it between the doll's legs.*

You know you like it.

> *SHE tosses the doll into the cauldron. The sound of an explosion. Smoke. SHE takes the lighter, considers burning the rope that binds her to the cauldron, but decides to light her own hair on fire instead. As she does so, lights dim on CHANTHAVY (HUMAN) and the cauldron.*
>
> *Lights up on MOTHER, who stands center stage, between the shadows of both Chanthavys. SHE holds her hands together (as in prayer) and bows her head at the audience, in greeting.*

MOTHER

Her name was Chanthavy, my moon child. Pale as the moon, white
like a pearl. So pure she could have passed for porcelain.

Lights up on Chanthavy (doll), at whom MOTHER nods.

Her future was bright. She was born smiling. Never cried when she
was starving. Never screamed when she was hurt.

That girl loved her father—maybe more than his due. She'd watched
as he'd festered, consumed with his disease. Those doctors said he'd
come too late. When he died and left us, she was five years old.

I traded a week's rice for a rag doll to see her smile.

She vowed to be a healer. She wrapped pretend bandages around the
rag doll's arms and legs. She fed it fake potions to make it strong.
Chanted spells in what she said was English. She loved that rag doll. I
loved my moon child.

Then one day she disappeared.

Lights fade on Chanthavy (doll).

I searched the playgrounds.

I searched the brothels.

I even went to the police.

Months later, a miracle: Two ladies brought her home. Human rights
ladies, foreign and clean. But my girl was not the same.

*Lights up on Chanthavy (human), at whom MOTHER
glares.*

Ugly. Filthy. Infected. Addicted to drugs. Shrieked, cursed. Messed
herself like a dog. Bit her baby sister on the cheek.

This was not my moon child. My girl was gone.

So I took this creature back to where they'd found her, and traded her for these shoes.

SHE stares down at her feet.

END OF SCENE 9

TRANSITION

WITCH 1 tosses her flip-flops into the cauldron as WITCHES 2 AND 3 appear. WITCH 2 sweeps up the mess. WITCH 3 takes a noose from the cauldron and ties it around Witch 1's neck as WITCH 1 transforms into Estrellita. As they perform these actions, the WITCHES chant:

Marwa Adly, age 21.
Vanished from the streets of Cairo, Egypt. 1998.

Mariane Magdi, age 18.
Vanished from the streets of Cairo, Egypt. 1998.

Rita Misien, age 19.
Vanished from the streets of Cairo, Egypt. 1998.

Theresa Ghattass Kamal, age 19.
Vanished from a village south of Cairo, Egypt. 2006.

Marian Bishay, age 15.
Vanished on her way to pick up dinner from a restaurant.
Giza, Egypt. 2009.

Heda Ebel, age 30.
Vanished while accompanying her son to school in a suburb of
Cairo, Egypt. 2011.

WITCHES 2 AND 3 vanish.

SCENE 10

LA CENICIENTA (PART 3)

Sometimes, when you cross a shipment of drugs to the United States, adrenaline is so high that you want to celebrate by killing women.

—an anonymous source to the *Dallas Morning News*,
February 28, 2004

CHARACTERS

ANGÉLICA	*12. Her factory smock is torn.*
ESTRELLITA	*16. A mannequin with a human head. SHE wears a witch mask and costume from the opening scene.*

SETTING

The desert and, deep within it, a puppet graveyard. The puppet graveyard is a wasteland strewn with masks, puppet pieces, and women's clothes and shoes. In a corner, the cauldron.

AT RISE

Stars twinkle. Then: moonlight. ESTRELLITA looms above the puppet graveyard like a rag doll. SHE is tied with rope, perhaps hanging from a noose, her head drooping. ANGÉLICA enters barefoot. SHE does not yet register the puppet graveyard.

ANGÉLICA

When I grow up, I want to be a princess. I want to dance all night and have magic—mice turn into handsome men and pumpkins into cars.

When I grow up, I want to live in a palace and have a room full of shoes. And socks.

And ice cream.

When I grow up, I want to be a ballerina who leaps up in the air and twirls 'round and 'round and 'round.

Or a bird who flies to the clouds.

And to Juárez.

And Durango.

I miss the donkeys but not the dirt.

> *ANGÉLICA stumbles over an item of clothing (Estrellita's blouse from scene 1). SHE picks it up and holds it up to the moonlight.*

A blouse? For a princess! And red is my favorite color.

> *SHE takes off the smock and puts on the blouse. As she dresses, SHE looks around and sees the clothes and shoes. SHE picks up a skirt (Estrellita's from scene 1).*

This skirt, so nice.

> *SHE puts on the skirt. SHE sees the puppet pieces but doesn't touch them. Suddenly she sees Estrellita.*

Dios mio!

> *SHE approaches Estrellita and studies her. ESTRELLITA raises her head, and her mask falls to the ground. ANGÉLICA jumps back.*

ESTRELLITA
That's my shirt.

ANGÉLICA

You are living! Then you can tell me where I am! You know how to get home—yes?

I tried to leave a trail of pebbles, but the grains of sand all look the same.

ESTRELLITA

And my skirt.

ANGÉLICA

If this is your skirt, what are you're wearing?

ESTRELLITA

They mixed up our clothes.

ANGÉLICA

But you are pretty.

ANGÉLICA kicks the witch mask away.

ESTRELLITA

Don't touch that.

ANGÉLICA approaches Estrellita to untie her.

I am Angélica. I will help you down.

ESTRELLITA

If you touch me, I'll break.

ANGÉLICA steps back and examines the puppet pieces on the ground. SHE picks up a puppet head and holds it tenderly.

ANGÉLICA

All these pieces. We must put them together.

SHE kisses the puppet head and places it back on the ground.

ESTRELLITA

All the king's horses, and all the king's men . . .

ANGÉLICA

You know that rhyme too? About the egg? Horses and men are too clumsy, but I will help you.

ESTRELLITA

Don't.

ANGÉLICA

Do you remember how la Cenicienta's sisters spilled the lentils to test her? They thought she could not pluck them out, but they were mistaken.

ESTRELLITA

The turtle doves plucked the lentils from the ashes. La Cenicienta couldn't do that.

ANGÉLICA

Maybe the doves will help us, too, and we will pass the test.

ESTRELLITA

We've already failed.

ANGÉLICA

What is your name?

ESTRELLITA

What difference does it make.

ANGÉLICA

Please tell me.

ESTRELLITA

Estrellita.

ANGÉLICA

Estrellita, little star. Listen to me, Estrellita: I jumped from the truck and raced away—even though I lost my shoes—like la Cenicienta when the clock struck twelve. If she can run barefoot, so can I. So can you. But . . . whose are these? These are cute.

SHE picks up a pair of red-laced sneakers (Estrellita's from scene 1) and puts them on.

These fit like a glass slipper.

ESTRELLITA

Those were mine, too.

ANGÉLICA

They suit my little feet.

ESTRELLITA

I loved red laces.

ANGÉLICA

I can put them on you. If you let me.

ESTRELLITA

I don't love them anymore.

ANGÉLICA

What we need is a pumpkin. What's in the pot?

Silence.

Aren't you curious?

ESTRELLITA

Curious? No. I want to know less. Un-know what I know now. Un-see what I've seen.

ANGÉLICA pops her head into the cauldron.

ANGÉLICA

> I hear water. Ocean waves and seagulls. This is the threshold. It's magic.

ESTRELLITA

> You're too old for fairy tales.

> > *ANGÉLICA smells the air above the cauldron.*

ANGÉLICA

> I smell sea mist, Estrellita. It's like happily-ever-after. We must go there.

> > *ANGÉLICA is about to climb into the cauldron.*

ESTRELLITA

> Angélica? Angélica! Wait!

> > *ANGÉLICA steps back. Suddenly, one of Estrellita's arms falls to the ground. ANGÉLICA shrieks.*

ANGÉLICA

> You are breaking!

> > *ANGÉLICA climbs onto the edge of cauldron.*

ESTRELLITA

> What are you doing?

ANGÉLICA

> Estrellita, I will fix you. I know I can fix you. I can untie you. I have little fingers. And a lot of patience. Oh yes, all of me is little. Except for my teeth. I have big teeth. Which Mamá says is why I will live forever.

> > *ANGÉLICA reaches for Estrellita's ropes.*

ESTRELLITA

> Don't do that! You'll fall in. Put my arm back on me.

> *ANGÉLICA stumbles and falls to the ground. A moment as she recovers. Then: one of Estrellita's legs falls off.*

ANGÉLICA

> *Dios mio!*

> *ANGÉLICA crawls to the leg and cradles it.*

ESTRELLITA

> Put me back together.

ANGÉLICA

> I am just a little girl.

ESTRELLITA

> Remember what you said: This is a test. Like la Cenicienta.

ANGÉLICA

> *(Rising up.)*
> That is true! I will help you, Estrellita. I will find the doves. I'll be fast. I'll run the whole way. I'll bring a doctor. A healer. A fairy godmother.

ESTRELLITA

> Take me with you.

> *ANGÉLICA climbs into the cauldron.*

ANGÉLICA

> We will pass this test. All you must do is believe. Say you believe.

ESTRELLITA

> I believe.

ANGÉLICA

> Now close your eyes and make a wish.

> *ESTRELLITA closes her eyes.*

I will wear your shoes. They will give me wings.

> *ANGÉLICA vanishes. ESTRELLITA's head droops.*
> *Darkness. Stars.*

ANGÉLICA
> *(Offstage, perhaps an echo.)*
> When I grow up, I want to be a princess.

> *ESTRELLITA raises her head and opens her eyes.*

ESTRELLITA
> Angélica?

> *Suddenly, the sound of a truck. Headlights shine on the*
> *cauldron. Angélica's Barbie doll descends from above, its*
> *head in a noose. It hangs suspended, illuminated by the*
> *headlights. Total darkness. Then: light up. WITCHES*
> *1, 2, AND 3 stand among the debris.*

ALL
> Jazmin Salazar Ponce, age 17.
> Vanished from Juárez, Mexico. December 27, 2010.
>
> Claudia Soto, age 19.
> Vanished from Juárez, Mexico. March 16, 2011.
>
> Nancy Iveth Navarro Muñoz, age 18.
> Vanished from Juárez, Mexico. July 13, 2011.
>
> Sara Martínez Morales, age 56.
> Vanished between Omealca and Tezonapa, Mexico. October 31, 2012.
>
> Jimena Jiménez Medalla, age 31.
> Vanished from Cuauhtémoc, Mexico. December 19, 2016.
>
> Maria Fernanda Sánchez Castillo, age 13.
> Vanished from Tepic, Mexico. November 5, 2018.
>
> Galilea Guadalupe Aguilar Palacio, age 16.
> Vanished from Manzanillo, Mexico. January 5, 2019.

Gabriela Vásquez Netro, age 27, and her five-year-old daughter. Vanished from Cerrito de la Cruz, Rayón, Mexico. January 15, 2019.

Karla Vanessa Martinez Turrubiartes, age 16, and her 11-month-old daughter. Vanished from San Luis Potosí, Mexico. January 27, 2019.

Nayeli Clemente Pérez, age 16. Vanished from Acatepec, Guerrero, Mexico. February 4, 2019.

Cinthia Belén Morales Juárez, age 24, and her three-month-old son. Vanished from Cazones, Veracruz, Mexico. March 8, 2019.

Ivonne Luna Ariza, age 21. Vanished from Orizaba, Veracruz, Mexico. March 12, 2019.

Yolanda González Covarrubias, age 32, and her 10-year-old son. Vanished from Xochimilco, Mexico. June 3, 2019.

Yamileth Abraján Villanueva, age 18, and her two-year-old son. Vanished from Acapulco, Mexico. August 13, 2019.

Guadalupe Wendolyn del Rió Cruz, age 23, and her six-year-old daughter. Vanished from Chihuahua, Mexico. August 21, 2019.

Sonia Arely Terrones Flores, age 29, and her nine-month-old son. Vanished from Tijuana, Mexico. October 8, 2019.

Guadalupe Flores Lucas, age 18. Vanished from Puerta del Sol de Tarimbaro, Michoacán, Mexico. October 16, 2019.

Dellany Paloma Reyes Escamilla, age 21. Vanished from Ziracuaretiro, Michoacán, Mexico. November 13, 2019.

END OF PLAY

WORKS CONSULTED

Ashilman, D. L., ed. and trans. "Little Red Riding Hood and Other Tales of Aarne-Thompson-Uther Type 333." Web.

Beinart, Haim. "Inés of Herrera del Duque: The Prophetess of Extremadura." In Giles 42-52.

Boeskorov, Gennady G. "Arctic Siberia: Refuge of the Mammoth Fauna in the Holocene." *Quaternary International* 142-143 (2006): 119-123.

Bullfinch, Thomas. *Bullfinch's Mythology.* Public Domain Books: Kindle, 2006.

Chartrand, Mark R. *National Audubon Society Field Guide to the Night Sky.* New York: Knopf, 1991.

A Decade of Dedication: Charter 77 1977-1987. New York: Helsinki Watch Committee: 1987.

Frazier, Ian. *Travels in Siberia.* New York: Farrar, 2010.

---. "Woolly." *The New Yorker* 10 Jan. 2011: 24-25.

Gheith, Jehanne M. and Katherine R. Jolluck, ed. *Gulag Voices: Oral Histories of Soviet Incarceration and Exile.* New York: Palgrave Macmillan, 2011.

Giles, Mary E., ed. *Women in the Inquisition: Spain and the New World.* Baltimore: Johns Hopkins, 1999.

Ginzburg, Eugenia Semyonovna. *Journey into the Whirlwind.* 1967. Trans. Paul Stevenson and Max Hayward. New York: Harvest, 1995.

Goetz-Stankiewicz, Marketa. *Good-bye, Samizdat: Twenty Years of Czechoslovak Underground Writing.* Evanston: Illinois UP, 1992.

Grimm, Jacob and Wilhelm. "Cinderella." 1857. *The Complete Fairy Tales of the Brothers Grimm.* Trans. Jack Zipes. New York: Bantam, 1987. 79-83.

Guillermoprieto, Alma. "Letter From Mexico: A Hundred Women: Why Has a Decade-Long String of Murders Gone Unsolved?" *The New Yorker* 30 Sept. 2003: 82-93.

Halliburton, Richard. *Seven League Boots: Adventures across the World from Arabia to Abyssinia.* 1935. Web.

Isom-Verhaaren, Christine. "Royal French Women in the Ottoman Sultans' Harem: The Political Uses of Fabricated Accounts from the Sixteenth to the Twenty-first Century." *Journal of World History* 17.2 (2006): 159-196.

Klíma, Ivan. "Guerilla Literature: Samizdat in the Age of Normalization." Faculty of the Arts, Charles University, Prague. 13 July 2010. Lecture.

Koren, Sharon Faye. "A Christian Means to a Converso End." *NASHIM: A Journal of Jewish Women's Studies and Gender Studies* 9 (2005): 27-61.

Mam, Somali with Ruth Marshall. *The Road of Lost Innocence: The True Story of a Cambodian Heroine.* New York: Spiegel & Grau, 2009.

Melammed, Renée Levine, ed. *Heretics or Daughters of Israel? The Crypto-Jewish Women of Castile.* Oxford: Oxford UP, 1999.

Nikolskiy, P.A., et al. "Prelude to Extinction: Revision of the Achchagyi Allaikha and Berelyokh Mass Accumulations of Mammoth." *Quaternary International* 219 (210): 16-25.

Nunes Carvalho, Solomon. "Rambles in Martinique." *Harper's New Monthly Magazine* Jan. 1874: 161-177.

Perrault, Charles. "Little Red Riding Hood." 1697. Trans. Andrew Lang. Web.

Phelan, Peggy. *Unmarked: The Politics of Performance.* New York: Routledge, 1993.

Rey, Debora. "Asteroid Named for Missing Argentine Student." *Tennessean* 24 Dec. 2011: 12A.

Rodriguez, Teresa. *The Daughters of Juárez: The True Story of Serial Murder South of the Border.* New York: Astria, 2007.

Salivarová, Zdena. *Summer in Prague.* 1972. Trans. Marie Winn. New York: Harper & Row, 1973.

Shakespeare, William. *The Tragedy of Macbeth.* 1623. *The Riverside Shakespeare.* Boston: Houghton Mifflin, 1974. 1312-1342.

Shalamov, Varlam. *Kolyma Tales.* Trans. John Glad. New York: Penguin, 1994.

Valdez, Diana Washington. *The Killing Fields: Harvest of Women.* Burbank: Peace at the Border, 2006.

The lists of names come from *The Killing Fields* and from numerous websites, including Project Disappeared, UNICEF, "Missing/Murdered Native Women in Canada," "Highway of Tears," Wikipedia, missing-persons databases, Facebook sites, and national and local news sources.